Baseball is Poetry in Motion

Ken Knee

Baseball is Poetry in Motion

Ken Knee

Copyright 2016 © by Ken Knee

ISBN 978-1-61529-169-4

Vision Publishing
1115 D Street
Ramona, CA 92065
1 800 9-VISION

All rights reserved.

No part of this book can be reproduced in any manner except by the written permission of the author except in brief quotations embodied in critical articles of review.

Introduction

Baseball is America's game. Although it is now played worldwide, we all know that the game's origin is right here in the USA. My father introduced me to the game when I was just a toddler. It's not surprising that his passion and enthusiasm for the game rubbed off onto me. Through the years I have followed the game with that same passion and enthusiasm and maybe even more so. I have tried to pass this zeal for the game on to my sons.

As I played baseball throughout my youth I became a student of the game. I use what I learned from that to understand and enjoy the game as a fan. Playing the game and being an active fan has also taught me the meaning of being competitive and has helped guide me through my life endeavors.

The game of baseball is descriptive of occurrences that we face in our everyday activities.

Baseball, like any other sport, teaches us to be competitive both at work and at play. Baseball furnishes us with discipline and also teaches us humility. At times it can be entertaining, exhilarating and humorous. On the other hand it can be dull and boring. Baseball is gratifying but it can be argumentative and dangerous. Because of the multitude of statistics and its rich history baseball is a marvelous educational tool. Everything that baseball offers helps build character in those who follow the game seriously.

Oh, yes, I almost forgot. Baseball is also dramatic, imaginative and romantic. All three of those words when used as adjectives are synonyms of poetic. Therefore, by logic, baseball is poetic. When you stop and think about that description for baseball you will understand the logic. Just about every motion of the players on the field is poetic in nature. It starts with the pitcher taking his windup, lifting his arm, striding towards home plate and then releasing the baseball. All of the pitchers action is poetry in motion.

A batter's swing – even if he misses the ball – is a poetic motion, maybe even more so when attempting to bunt. A player fielding a batted ball may be the most poetic motion in all of baseball. Think about all of the incredible defensive plays you've seen. Each and every one has a poetic motion whether the player is diving for a ball, leaping against the wall to pull down a possible home run or turning the double play at second base. Even routine plays have their own poetic motions. Then there's players running and sliding into a base. And, yes, even umpires have their own unique way of poetry in motion with the way they punch a batter out on a called third strike or on the base paths.

Since baseball and poetry are synonymous – at least in my eyes - I have written this book of baseball related poems for my enjoyment as well as yours. Before you read this book I must warn you that I was born and raised on Chicago's north side so I was destined to become a lifetime Cubs fan. Therefore, quite a number of verses relate to Chicago Cub players and history. Don't hold it against me that I'm a Cubs fan and don't feel sorry for me. It's my choice and I have to live with it. Enjoy the book.

Ken Knee

Dedication

This book is dedicated to my father, Manuel Knee, who died at sixty-one – way too soon
Whenever they play that song about baseball I think of him – how he loved that tune
You know the one about buying some peanuts and cracker jack
And when we went to a ballgame we didn't care if we ever got back

Oh, how he used to tell me such great stories about the players of times gone by
Ruth, Gehrig, Cobb, Wilson, Hornsby, Wagner, Johnson and a guy named Cy
It was a sad day when the Lord took him to that big place in the sky
Oh, how I miss him – I'm so sorry I never got to say goodbye

The most important player in major league history was George Herman Ruth, also known as Babe Ruth or just simply as 'The Babe'. Besides being a great baseball player, Ruth was also a very colorful person. Because of his notoriety, what better way to begin the Official Book of Baseball Poetry than with a tribute to 'The Babe.'

THE BABE

Babe Ruth saved baseball so the legend goes
He made everyone forget about the Black Sox woes
He was the first of the really true power hitters
Just striding to the plate gave pitchers the jitters

His career started as a pitcher with the Red Sox
Then he got traded to that team in the Bronx
They quickly turned him into an everyday player
He became so popular he could have run for Mayor

His legend grew with every home run
But 'The Babe' was more for having fun
He would chase women and party all night
And from time to time get into a fight

But at game time he was always ready to go
To take his place among Murderer's Row
'Cause with 'The Babe' it was all about the game
That's why he's a charter member of the Hall of Fame

Then there was the time that he called his shot
It was against the Cubs who claimed he did not
'The Babe' cleared the fence with a tremendous blow
Oh, how that man really knew how to put on a show

There have been numerous changes to the game throughout the decades. For the most part the changes have been good for the game. Rule changes are usually meant to improve the game and for the most part they do. However changes and personal decisions that are out of control have been a detriment to the game. But the game will survive because it is too big not too. Some of the latest changes are mentioned below.

WHAT'S HAPPENING TO THE GAME?

They're tearing down the Cathedrals of baseball
Yankee Stadium and Shea are the latest to fall
Their replacements are decidedly state of the art
But the costs are as shocking as a dagger to the heart

Today's player salaries are totally out of sight
Blame the owners, they created their own blight
And how about the price they charge for a beer
And they keep raising it year after year

The state of the game has become quite a mess
But the fans keep hoping for a miracle, God Bless
They keep coming out because they love the game
To them it doesn't matter who or what is to blame

Attendance is way up all over the place
Even if the team isn't in a pennant race
The steroid scandal hasn't chased anyone away
That high price for tickets fans are willing to pay

They've added instant replay to help get things right
That's almost as scary as things that go bump in the night
The strike zone keeps changing from ump to ump
Sometimes they make a hitter look like a chump

What's happening to the game, the game we all love

The game the compassionate fans put nothing else above
But wait avid baseball fans, show some confidence
Fenway and Wrigley still stand, leveling them makes no sense

There have been so many rivalries in major league baseball throughout the decades that you can't name them all. So why even try. However the Cubs and Braves rivalry dates back to 1876 to form the oldest rivalry in baseball.

THE OLDEST RIVALRY

The Cubs and Braves rivalry goes back to what seems like before time began
The rivalry is so old it seems like it was created before the first baseball fan
These two teams were members of the National League in eighteen seventy-six
That was in the days when baseball bats were known as sticks

In current day the media pushes the great rivalry of the Yankees and Red Sox
But that rivalry doesn't even go as far back as England's hunting of the fox
They just promote that competitive rivalry to sell more newspapers
But the Cubs and Braves go back to when baseball was still in diapers

Back in eighteen seventy-six both teams played under a different name
That wasn't all that was different – so was the way they played the game
The Cubs were known as the 'White Stockings' and a lot of games they won
While the Braves were called the 'Red Caps' and played out of Boston

When the Braves were in Milwaukee the rivalry became rather heated
The Braves were very good then which meant the Cubs were usually defeated

Today, with the Braves in Atlanta, a lot of miles separate the two teams
But the rivalry continues and the fans are still enthused or so it seems

Rogers Hornsby was one of the greatest players in baseball history. He was also one of the most detestable persons to ever play the game. When I was a young boy of eight I met the man at a baseball dinner. To me he seemed like a nice person and I was thrilled to know him once I found out who he was.

"RAJAH"

Rogers Hornsby was the greatest right hand hitter to ever play the game
It was a no brainer when it came time to elect him to the Hall of Fame
His career was winding down when he came to the Cubs in twenty-nine
He hit a robust three eighty to top a fantastic statistical line

The three eighty batting average is still a Cubs franchise record for a season
That was his only good year with the Cubs as his career was just about done
He was named manager of the Cubs but he didn't get along with anyone
Many of the players complained that playing for him wasn't any fun

Hornsby played for the rival St. Louis Cardinals for twelve years
So Cub fans were accustomed to giving Hornsby plenty of jeers
His lack of a winning personality didn't endear him to Cub devotees
But they put up with him because of his tremendous baseball abilities

When I was eight-years old I met Hornsby at a Little League dinner
I sat next to him at the head table because I was an award winner
I had no idea who the man was except that he was old and gray
But my dad knew who he was and just talking to him made his day

Everyone likes a game where a lot of runs are scored. Baseballs are falling safe all day or night long. However, the true connoisseur of the game loves a low scoring, well-pitched game. And even more so when a number of spectacular defensive plays occur. There have been many great pitchers in the game but I never saw anyone better than Sandy Koufax. The poem below is an example of his mastery.

I LOVE THIS GAME

I woke up this morning with a terrible itch
I wanted to go see Koufax pitch
So I told my boss 'I'm taking the day off'
'I'm not feeling well, got a really bad cough'

It was a gorgeous day, not a cloud in the sky
What more could a fan want for mid-July
As game time neared the excitement grew
The crowd couldn't wait to see Koufax in Dodger blue

Top of the first Koufax struck out the side
They had no chance of hitting that horsehide
Second inning he struck out one more
That brought his game total to four

The third, fourth and fifth Koufax kept rolling along
Striking out five more he could do nothing wrong
At the end of the sixth neither team had scored
The sellout crowd was starting to get bored

In the seventh the Dodgers dented the plate
Koufax singled home Roseboro his battery mate
Into the ninth Koufax took his 1-0 lead
Just three more outs that's all he would need

Koufax had the leadoff hitter in a 0-2 hole
You just knew that striking him out was his goal
Koufax took his windup and hummed a fastball

The umpire raised his arm strike three was the call

The next batter cautiously stepped into the box
Koufax broke off a curve he swung out of his socks
He tried to hit the next pitch out of sight
He was retired on a lazy fly ball to right

One out to go so the crowd rose to their feet
They could sense that Koufax has these guys beat
Then the crowd started to yell 'strike this guy out'
I thought to myself 'that's what this game is all about'

In baseball the word defense is synonymous with shortstop supreme Ozzie Smith. The 'Wizard of Oz' as he was known would make unbelievable defensive plays that no human being should be able to make. And what was even more amazing was that he made it look easy.

THE WIZARD

Watching Ozzie Smith perform his fielding wizardry was a pleasure
His work with the glove created memories we will always treasure
Every fan delighted at his marvelous defensive skills
He would constantly provide them with acrobatic defensive thrills

His early years in The Show attested he was no wizard with the stick
But with hard work and perseverance his offensive game started to click
In '87 his game peeked with a batting average of .303, a career high
During his career he stole five hundred and eighty bases, wow could he fly

Ozzie played the game with dedication, determination, and a lot of desire
He was full of energy and when he stepped on the field he seemed on fire
His first inning back flip created excitement before the game began
And his on field game accomplishments delighted every baseball fan

The Chicago Cubs have had so many years of futility we don't want to go into it here. However, the futility aside, the Cubs have had a good number of players enter the Hall of Fame. Among them is Mr. Cub, Ernie Banks. Banks is probably the most important Chicago Cub is their long history. Below is a tribute to Mr. Cub.

MR.CUB

If you were born and raised a Chicago Cubs' fan
To you Ernie Banks has always been the man
'Let's play two' he would always shout
And he would never sit still for a rainout

In the sixties he was the life of the team
And when he'd homer everyone would beam
Ernie handled every home run with style
As he crossed home plate he would always smile

Because of his charisma and good nature
The fans called him 'Mr. Cub' instead of sir
'Mr. Cub' was the absolute perfect name
It showed the respect of his baseball fame

One thing about his career that was really sad
He played on Cubs' teams that were really bad
This deprived him of a hunger and career ambition
A World Series appearance never came to fruition

The 50's was probably the greatest decade in the history of baseball. There were so many exciting games and it was the players who made it so. There were so many great players from that decade that went into the Hall of Fame that it would be an impossible task to remember them all. Besides Banks, there was Aaron, Musial, Williams, Mathews, Doby, Campanella, the three Robinsons, Reese, Rizzuto, Slaughter, Berra and on and on. And I haven't even mentioned the pitchers or the first names of the above because you know them all. Oh, yes, let's not forget those three centerfielder's that played in New York ... .

WILLIE, MICKEY AND THE DUKE

New York was the best place to be in the fifty's if you loved baseball
Every year one or more of the teams would still be playing in the fall
The Giants, Yankees and Dodgers were the names of the teams
They would play to sellout crowds every game or so it seems

The Giants played in the Polo Grounds located in Queens
Their manager Durocher would win games by any means
Their star centerfielder was a kid named Willie Mays
He was so good that he could beat you in so many ways

Willie would perform legendary baseball feats beyond reason
And he kept doing it game after game, season after season
Giants' fans stormed the gates to see Willie play
Whenever he'd do something great they'd yell 'Say Hey'

The Yankees played across the river and were called the 'Bronx Bombers'
That's because they had power hitters who hit homers by the numbers
Yankee fans were spoiled because they had such a winning tradition
That's because their everyday lineup was loaded with ammunition

A kid from Oklahoma named Mickey swung their most potent bat
He hit many a prodigious blow which proved he was one cool cat
Mickey Mantle was the best switch hitter the game has ever known
It seemed when he stepped to the plate he was in a special zone

The Dodgers played at Ebbets Field in Brooklyn's Flatbush section
The fans came out to root for the 'Bums' and have lots of fun
It was a great Dodger team that played at that old ball yard
And 'The Duke' patrolled centerfield like a palace guard

In fifty five the Dodgers managed to win a World Series title
And Duke Snider's four home runs in the series were vital
'The Duke' didn't get as much attention as Willie and Mickey
But he was popular with Dodger fans from A to Z

All three left their mark in different ways in the game of baseball
That's why it was a no brainer to elect them all to the Hall
If you would poll the fans as to whom was the most exciting
The answer would depend in which borough you were standing

Power hitting centerfielders do not come along every day so New York baseball fans in the fifties were very privileged to have three of them at the same time. Another power hitting centerfielder who played briefly for the Dodgers was Lewis 'Hack' Wilson. Here is his story.

BATTLIN' HACK WILSON

At five-foot-six, 200 pounds, Hack Wilson's physique was roly-poly
Being almost as wide as he was tall he should have been a hockey goalie
With his barrel chest and stubby legs he looked less like an athlete than Princess Grace
But he could hit a baseball and amongst the greats of the game he took his place

Born Lewis Robert Wilson in 1900, Hack was raised in Pennsylvania steel country
He developed his strength by swinging heavy hammers for a locomotive company
Hack started out a catcher and had three good seasons in the minors but was deemed too short
However John McGraw signed him for New York where in the outfield he would cavort

Hack became a Cub in twenty-six and had five very productive years
But his demise came about because he just drank too many beers
His drinking and carousing kept him up late most nights
And his bad temper got him into on and off the field fights

In 1930 Hack hit 56 homers and drove in 191 runs in a season for the ages
But all that success still didn't stop him from going into drunken rages

Cubs' management wouldn't put up with him anymore and sent him packing
Because of his problems he played four more seasons with his ability lacking

After playing for St. Louis and Brooklyn he was out of baseball after thirty-four
His statistics were bad, his attitude the same, nobody wanted him anymore
Wilson could have been one of the greatest but drinking was his downfall
Even still, the baseball writers thought enough of him to elect him to the Hall

The Chicago Cubs are the oldest franchise in baseball dating back to the 1870's. Over those 140 plus years many interesting and unusual things have occurred. Some were good. Some were bad and others were really bad. The short items below take us in a time travel back into Cubs' history.

LONG, LONG AGO

Long, long ago the Cubs were a consistent winning team
They would win the pennant ever year or so it would seem
That was the 19th century and they were known as the White Stockings
Owners were frugal back then and didn't give out championship rings

MENDOZA LINE

In 1981 the Cubs had four infielders that hit below the Mendoza line
Instead of playing every day these guys should have been riding the pine
Or even better they should have been shipped out to the farm
Replaced by little leaguers, what would have been the harm

A TRIPLE TRIPLE

In sixty-five the Cubs turned three triple plays
No surprise they had an all-star infield those days
On the mound for all three of them was Bill Faul
Now there's an accomplishment worthy of the Hall

POPEYE

Don Zimmer's managing decisions weren't always by the book
But he was all about winning no matter what it took

Doing the unconventional seemed to work for him
He kept the fans on edge anticipating his every whim

ERRORS PART OF THE GAME

Roy Smalley led the league in errors one year
Oh boy, did the Cubs' shortstop hear the fans jeer
Every game the problem wouldn't go away
A vitamin was named after him – One-A-Day

DUSTIN' OFF ERNIE

Knocking down Ernie Banks was a big mistake
It was as if an alarm went off and he would awake
In fifty-seven four pitchers tried to leave their mark
Each time Ernie hit the next pitch out of the park

NOLES FOR NOLES

The Cubs traded a pitcher to Detroit in eighty-seven by the name of Dickie Noles
He was traded for a pitcher to be named so the Cubs could fill some future holes
After pitching in four games the Tigers decided he didn't fit into any of their roles
So they traded him back to the Cubs and the player to be named was Dickie Noles

PADRE BLITZ

In sixty-nine the newly formed Padres visited Wrigley and ran into a buzz saw
The Cubs tied a team shutout record that day when they laid down the law

The Cubs laced up their hitting shoes and blitzed the Padres nineteen to zero
Everybody chipped in with Ernie Banks driving in seven runs being the hero

LEO 'THE LIP'

Leo Durocher was hired to bring law and order to the Cubs' dugout
His fiery personality and leadership ability provided a ton of clout
But alas, like everywhere else he went he wore out his welcome
No matter what his success fans will remember him as just another bum

SLUGFEST

In twenty-two the Cubs and Phillies got involved in a slugfest
As the game went on nobody knew who was coming out best
Walks, hits and runs were cheap, easy and free
The Cubs won the game twenty-six to twenty-three

CUBS AND PHILLIES AGAIN

Another slugfest in '79 with the player's different but teams the same
No power outage as there was twenty-three extra base hits in the game
The final score was twenty-three to twenty-two with the Phillies winning
And wouldn't you know there were runs scored in just about every inning

ALL-TIME CUBS OUTFIELD

Billy Williams, Hack Wilson and Sammy Sosa in left, center and right
That's the Cubs' all-time outfield 'cause they could all hit the ball out of sight
Between them they hit 1,279 homers with Sosa hitting almost half
If anyone disputes this trio just smile, look them in the face and laugh

NO 4-HOMER GAMES FOR A CUB

No Cub has ever hit four home runs in a single game
Many have hit three which doesn't put them too shame
Come to think of it four home runs in a game is an awesome feat
Maybe someday a Cub player will do it, wouldn't that be neat

THE BAD CUBS

In the late seventy's the Cubs were a bad team and among the missing
Many times during that era it was assumed they had all gone fishing
Most games they played so bad it left even the die-hard fans wishing
That the whole team would take the season off and really go fishing

WE SURRENDER

In May of sixty-seven the Cubs beat up on the Dodgers
It was so bad they couldn't have been rescued by Roy Rogers
The Cubs won the game twenty to three – from the beginning it was a rout

During the game the Dodgers were waving white towels from the dugout

SOUTHPAW CRISIS

In sixty-three Dick Ellsworth became the fifth Cubs' lefty to win twenty games
Except for Hippo Vaughn – who did it five times – the others were no names
There must be some sort of curse that the Cubs can't develop a premier southpaw
After further review it isn't a curse but more of a serious development flaw

BIG LOSER FOR A WINNER

Only one pitcher has lost as many as 19 games for a pennant winner
And had a losing record to boot but not once was he late for dinner
In thirty-eight a ten and nineteen record was hung on Larry French
Even though the Cubs won the pennant he created quite a stench

TOOTHPICK SAM

Sam Jones chomped ferociously on his toothpick as he looked in for the sign
It was the top of the ninth, he had a no-hitter working but the game was on the line
He had loaded the bases on walks as he lost control and every pitch was wide
He bore down and preserved the no-hitter as he proceeded to strike out the side

Growing up in Chicago was a wonderful experience. In the fall and winter we had the Bears and mounds of snow. In the spring and summer we had the Cubs and high humidity. Of course, we didn't have the Cubs in the fall because ..... well, you know why. Also, a major part of growing up in Chicago was ......

GROWING UP WRIGLEY

More than fifty years have passed so now the story can be told
How we used to cut school on game day – wow we were bold
The high school we attended was just four blocks from the El
We would take off early never waiting for that final bell

The train ride to the park was fast and only cost a dime
That's why we would always get to our seats by game time
Those were the days – bleacher seats were only twenty-five cents
We'd sit in left waiting for Banks to hit one or two over the fence

It was the late fifties and the Cubs were really bad
Sometimes they played so awful it made us mad
But we didn't care – it beat going to school by a mile
And besides it was baseball – major league style

The Cubs had a pitching staff that nobody could forget
There was 'Who's He,' 'Send Him Packing', and 'He's All Wet'
They weren't very good but they were sure entertaining
They kept hanging curve balls like it was still spring training

But this was Wrigley Field – baseball's number one place
Who cared that the Cubs were never in the pennant race
We were there to cheer and hope the Cubs could save face
And also to escape that incredibly fast high school pace

In those days 'Growing Up Wrigley' was the thing to do
It beat running around with every Tom, Dick and Sue
Just getting out in the spring time and breathing fresh air
Whatever the consequences were we didn't care

One day our principal called us into his office for a meeting
We cut it short so we wouldn't miss our game time seating
He considered locking us up and throwing away the key
He even threatened to move our classrooms to Wrigley

But 'Growing Up Wrigley' wasn't just all about baseball
Watching the Cubs taught us about adversity and how to stand tall
So you see, 'Growing Up Wrigley' was a once in a lifetime experience
It's been fifty years and I miss it – nothing has been the same ever since

Throughout the years baseball and its fans have experienced many exciting moments. Great defensive plays, timely clutch hitting, and overpowering pitching have delighted us. There have been so many great moments that no one can remember them all in their lifetime. Just about every extraordinary play has induced the crowd to jump to their feet and cheer with delight. I'm sure everyone has a favorite play or moment they have seen whether it was made by their favorite team or by the opposition. It's something that stays with you and you remember it forever. In my many years of watching and observing baseball I have seen so many great plays and have had quite a few other baseball moments that it would be impossible to remember them all. I still remember great moments that occurred as far back as the early 50's. If I had to pick out a top ten from all those special moments and put it in writing it would be as follows. Although I didn't witness all of them first hand, the fans that did sure got enjoyment when they happened.

MY TEN MOST EXCITING BASEBALL MOMENTS

The most exciting action in baseball is defense, defense, and more defense
Like watching outfielders leap up and catch a ball against the fence
Number 10 on my list is a defensive play made by outfielder Bo Jackson
After a long run and making the catch I still can't believe what he had done
To avoid a collision with another outfielder he jumped and ran on the wall
He took two steps and then landed on the ground and still held on to the ball

Another outstanding defensive play is on my list at number nine
It was so great that is was better than a hundred- year-old aged wine

In game one of the 1954 World Series there was a major defensive event
Willie Mays made 'The Catch' that many Giant fans still call it God sent
The Indian's Vic Wertz hit a ball to deep center that Mays plucked out of the air
He caught the ball with his back to the infield, a feat that is so very rare

Hitting four hundred over a full major league season is a feat beyond reason
In 1941 Ted Williams was the last to hit four hundred over a full season
On the last day of the season Williams' average was sitting at three-nine-nine point five-five
That's hitting four hundred so his manager told him to sit so the average wouldn't take a dive
Williams insisted on playing both games of a doubleheader that day to seal his fate
He had six hits and finished as four-hundred-six – on my list that's number eight

Kirk Gibson's dramatic World Series home run comes in at number seven
When he hit it every Dodger fan was sure it was his ticket to heaven
An aching Gibson limped and pumped his arm as he rounded the bases
The whole team met him at home plate with a smile on their faces
The fact that Gibson could hardly walk made the home run a memorable event
It makes one wonder if it was possibly heaven sent

Number six is a record established by Cincinnati Reds pitcher Johnny Vander Meer
In 1938 he threw two consecutive no-hitters and it was his rookie year

No pitcher in the history of the game has been able to match this feat
And this is one record that no major league pitcher will be able to delete
Pitching a no hitter is like finding gold at the end of a rainbow
To break this record a pitcher would have to throw three in a row

Branch Rickey was one of the most innovative men in baseball history
What he did in 1947 made headlines and was certainly no mystery
Jackie Robinson became the first black man to play major league baseball
Because of the times almost everybody in baseball thought Rickey had a lot of gall
It caused a lot of unrest and Robinson was lucky to make it through the season alive
Because of this monumental and important event it made my list at number five

Once Robinson broke the color line no one had any idea what the future would be
Soon there were others that followed Robinson's arduous journey
Larry Doby, Roy Campanella and Don Newcombe immediately after
When the fans saw these guys could play the jeers turned to laughter
Then in the fifty's another great group such as Banks and Aaron came along
These guys were so good that the fans shouted that they could do no wrong

If someone would have told me Aaron would do what he did I would have shown them the door
But he broke Ruth's career home run record and that's why my list has Aaron at number four
It was a night game in Atlanta when Aaron hit number 715 off of Dodger lefty Al Downing

The crowd was cheering, the stadium was rocking, but poor Al Downing was frowning
Most purists still believe Aaron is the all time home run leader because he stayed clean
And all his fans will tell you he's the best home run hitter they've ever seen

1956 World Series, Game 5, Yankee right hander Don Larsen threw a perfect game
The rest of his career was mediocre at best so this was his claim to fame
Yankee catcher Yogi Berra ran out and jumped in his arms when he recorded the final out
Larsen had pin-point control that day and the final outcome was never in doubt
This is number three on my list even though baseball historians might rank it higher
But this is my list and this ranking is what I desire

In 1951 the Giants' Bobby Thomson hit a walk-off home run that was borough shocking
Giant fans stood and jeered - they couldn't believe it – the Polo Grounds was rocking
Brooklyn was ahead 4-2 when Dodger pitcher Ralph Branca looked in to get the sign
It was the ninth inning and two runners were on base – the playoffs were on the line
Branca delivered, Thompson swung, and the fans in the left field stands had a wonderful view
The ball landed over the fence and the Giants won the pennant and on my list this is number two

Number one on my list is easy as it's all about 'The Greatest Home Run Ever'
Bill Mazeroski hit a home run that baseball fans will remember forever

It was the 1960 World Series, ninth inning of game 7, and the score was tied
Ralph Terry was on the mound and Mazeroski gave his pitch a long ride
The Pirates team celebrated by running out on the field
The entire Yankee team knew that their loss had been sealed

Although experiencing the pleasantries that Wrigley Field has brought, being a Cubs' fan has been very frustrating to say the least. However, we Cub fans find a way to keep going and look for some light as the end of the tunnel. Let me explain what it's been like.

SIXTY PLUS YEARS AND COUNTING

The Cubs won the pennant in forty-five when I was four-years-old
Ever since then I've cheered hard but watched them fold
It's been sixty plus frustrating years and I'm still counting
As the years go by I grow weary but my hopes keep mounting

There have been many years where the team has given me hope
But somehow they always fail and I've learned to cope
In eighty-four it looked like we could go all the way
But it was not to be as the Padres had their say

In two thousand and three we were five outs away from the promise land
Again not to be as lady luck stepped in and dealt a really bad hand
Then Piniella came along and things were looking bright
But after a short time even he couldn't get it right

Don't get me wrong. There was a lot of enjoyment over the years. The Cubs had some Hall of Fame players besides Ernie Banks and Hack Wilson pass through the Wrigley Field Portals. The recent ones were ....

SWEET SWINGIN' BILLY

Billy Williams was such a pure hitter that word was he could hit in the dark
And if you turned on the lights he would probably hit it out of the park
When it came to hitting a baseball Billy had all of the essentials
That's why Cub fans knew he had Hall of Fame credentials

Billy won National League rookie of the year honors in sixty-one
While romping in the Cubs' outfield and playing every day in the sun
And while on the subject of playing in the sun every day
Billy played in 1,117 consecutive games while earning his pay

During much of his career he played with Banks, Jenkins and Santo
But they couldn't make it to the post season adding to Cub fans woe
Billy won the batting title in seventy-two when he hit three-thirty-three
With his other great statistics his not winning the MVP was a travesty

But Billy got his due when he was elected to the Hall of Fame
Final proof that Billy Williams really knew how to play this game
Billy made his debut with the Cubs in '59 and played for them through '74
The Cubs traded him and it was hard going to Wrigley and not seeing him anymore

SANTO BLED CUBS BLUE

Ron Santo is and has been a Chicago Cub through and through
If you had ever asked him he would say he bleeds Cubs blue
Since his retirement from the game he became a die-hard Cubs fan
And he saw every game from the press box as the radio broadcast color man

Santo arrived on the scene in the early sixties and made an immediate impact
His timely hitting and smooth fielding made him a fan favorite, that's a fact
He teamed with Banks and Williams to form the Cubs version of Murderer's Row
This attracted the fans as they knew that the threesome would put on a show

Santo played his entire career with a deep dark secret that nobody knew
As a youngster he was diagnosed a diabetic, because of it his determination grew
Tho' he was slow afoot he led the league in triples in sixty-four with thirteen
Watching him run the bases and sliding into a base usually caused quite a scene

With four straight years with home runs over thirty he proved he was mighty
And he was an RBI machine with eight straight years of more than ninety
Most important of all is that Santo really loved to play the game
It took some time but he finally made it to the Hall of Fame

SPLIT FINGER BRUCE

Bruce Sutter resurrected his career with the development of the split-finger fastball
His accomplishments with that one pitch alone sealed his election to the Hall
Sutter spent the first five years of his career playing on Chicago's north side
He led the league in saves the last two years giving Cub fans quite a ride

His tenure with the Cubs was in an era when they languished in the second division
But just watching him close out a victory in those days was probably the most fun
Sutter's career was cut short because of problems with his pitching arm
It was said the split-finger pitch he developed caused him the most harm

THE INTIMIDATOR

I call Fergie Jenkins 'The Intimidator' because he was our answer to Bob Gibson
Ask anyone who faced him and they'd say, "Hitting against him wasn't fun."
Ferguson Jenkins had his best years with the Cubs with his forte being his control
He won twenty games six straight seasons because throwing strikes was his goal

Fergie's control led to his dominating opponent hitters of any kind
He struck out over 3,000 as they swung at pitches as if they were blind
He won 24 games and the coveted Cy Young award in seventy-one

That was with most of his games being played under the hot
    Chicago sun

Just stepping out on the mound would start his competitive juices
    to flow
As the game went on his determination would cause the other team
    woe
Fergie knew how to pitch and he knew how to get the other team
    out
He won 284 games and was one of the best of his era without a
    doubt

After '73 he was traded to the American League for a guy named
    Madlock
The first year he won 25 games showing the other league he was a
    rock
Fergie got the call from the Hall of Fame in ninety-one
His induction was the final reward for all he had done

RYNO

A player the caliber of Ryne Sandberg comes along once in a …
    well, a millennium
And his performances like the Sandberg game in '84 has left the
    fans totally numb
To think the Cubs got him as a throw-in in the DeJesus for Bowa
    trade
After struggling as a third baseman nobody thought he'd make the
    grade

Instead of sending him for more minor league seasoning down on
    the farm
He switched to second base and became a smooth fielder with a
    strong arm
In the field Sandberg wasn't flashy but he was consistent and very
    steady

He was deft at fielding anything hit his way because he was always ready

Ryno won nine gold gloves and there were numerous fielding records that he set
His bat came alive in '84 as he sparked a pennant drive no Cub fan can ever forget
He won the MVP that year when he dominated in almost every offensive category
He led the league in runs scored and triples and that was only the beginning of his glory

Because of his popularity, Ryno should be labeled Mr. Cub of his generation
Just like the original Mr. Cub, Ernie Banks, it was all about determination
Ryno slugged 282 lifetime homers but was better known for his total offensive game
And we wonder why it wasn't until his third try that he was elected to the Hall of Fame

I think of the good old days of baseball being before 1950. The Cubs had some great ball players during those good old days. Hack Wilson was probably the best of them but some old time Cub fans would argue Cap Anson, Gabby Hartnett or Three-Finger Brown were just as good, even better than Wilson. Here is a tribute to those great old-timers.

"GABBY"

Gabby Hartnett was the best catcher in NL history before Johnny Bench came along
He was the prototypical catcher who in Cub fans eyes could do no wrong
Even though Gabby is best known for his 'Homer in the Gloamin'
His catching and hitting prowess made him a classic baseball showman

That home run was hit in '38 against Pittsburgh late on a September afternoon
It gave the Cubs a ninth inning victory and the pennant as fans jumped to the moon
It is still the most important home run in Chicago Cubs history
How Gabby saw that pitch in the darkness is still a mystery

Gabby was the catcher when Carl Hubbell put on that great all-star game show
In the '34 game Hubbell struck out Ruth, Gehrig, Foxx, Simmons and Cronin in a row
In thirty-five Gabby won the National League Most Valuable Player award
He hit .344 that year with 91 runs batted in and to new heights his popularity soared

For those who haven't figured it out, he got his nickname from his constant chatter
Behind home plate he would constantly talk with the intent on unnerving the batter

Gabby's most important accomplishment was his election to the Hall of Fame
He is a Cubs legend and it will always be remembered that he ran as if he were lame

THREE FINGER

Moredecai 'Three-Finger' Brown became a Hall of Fame pitcher by chance
An accident when he was a kid distorted his hand and his grip made the ball dance
Brown lost half of his index finger and had other injuries to the hand on his pitching arm
This happened when he tangled with a corn chopper on his uncle's Indiana farm

The unnatural grip he used on the ball made it move in peculiar directions
Hitters had a devil of a time hitting his pitches because of the reactions
'Three-Finger' had six straight years when he won 20 games or more
Five of those years his ERA was under two, he would show batters the door

His lifetime earned run average was 2.06, one of the best in the game
That statistic proved that time after time he put hitters to shame
Brown was a key member of the Cubs' last championship team
With all the innings he pitched he never ran out of steam

TINKER TO EVERS TO CHANCE

Tinker to Evers to Chance was the double play combo of nineteen-O-eight
But really how good were these guys together? That's the debate

Although none of them had great stats they were a natural fit
In '46 all three were elected to the Hall of Fame as a unit

Joe Tinker and Evers didn't get along and had a 25-year feud
Tinker didn't talk to Evers because of his irascible mood
Tinker was by far the best fielder of the trio
Everything hit to him seemed to fit into a flow

Johnny Evers had a nervous and almost insane disposition
Just being around him would throw you into depression
But for all his shortcomings Evers knew the rules of the game
And his participation in the Merkle Incident brought him fame

Besides playing first base Frank Chance was the Cubs manager
It was under his leadership and guidance that made the team purr
Chance was a great base runner and is the Cubs all-time stolen base leader
His all around baseball ability and knowledge made him a world beater

'CAP'TAIN

Twenty-seven consecutive years is a major league record for the game
That and the first to three thousand hits was Adrian Anson's claim to fame
He was dubbed 'Cap' because he was the team captain and they also called him 'Pops'
Of all the great hitters in the nineteenth century he was the tops

Cap Anson was a competitor to the highest regard
And as team Captain he drilled his teammates hard
He was an innovator and credited with developing the "Hit and Run"
He taught his teammates the play to win ball games not for having fun

Cap holds so many hitting records there isn't enough space to list them here
He kept leading the league in different categories and did so year after year
He was elected to the Hall of Fame by the veteran's committee in thirty-nine
It was an easy choice for them after they reviewed his statistical line

Excuse the pun but Anson has one black mark against his name
He led a faction that didn't allow dark-skinned players into the game
When Jackie Robinson appeared I'm sure Anson was spinning in his grave
I guess Anson felt a dark-skinned person was not a ballplayer but a slave

Pete Rose has been denied entry into the Hall because of his gambling weakness

And others haven't been considered for their assumed part of the steroid mess
But isn't racial bias in today's society a much bigger crime than those
Then why is Cap Anson in the Hall of Fame? That's the question I pose

Besides having those great Hall of Fame ballplayers, the Cubs have had seven Most Valuable Player and four Cy Young award winners. Some of them are in the Hall of Fame and they have been mentioned above. Here is a poetic tribute to all of these award winners.

THE MVP'S

The baseball writers created the MVP award back in thirty-one
To honor the best player who cavorted under the afternoon sun
Over the years seven Cubs have won this prestigious award
After having great seasons they were bestowed with this reward

Gabby Hartnett was the first Cub to win it – that was in thirty-five
He hit a whopping .344 that year as his bat really came alive
Gabby was 34 that year – old for a catcher – but still in his prime
Two years later he almost won the award for a second time

Ten years later – 1945 – Phil Cavaretta was awarded the MVP
He had a year that looked like he was hitting off a batting tee
His .355 average led the Cubs to the National League crown
This left little doubt that Phil was the main man in Chitown

In 1952 the MVP award went to Cubs' left fielder Hank Sauer
Now there was a guy who could really hit for power
Sauer led the league in home runs and RBI's that season
To NL pitchers his bat was as lethal as a loaded gun

Mr. Cub, Ernie Banks, won the award in fifty-eight and fifty-nine
His performance those years was better than the taste of an
    expensive wine
Ernie slugged 47 home runs and drove in 129 runs in fifty-eight
But the Cubs struggled as a team and a losing season was their fate

In fifty-nine, Ernie had an even bigger year with 45 homers and
    143 RBI's
He also hit .304 that year which brought a lot of "Oh me, oh mys"
But as a team the Cubs were again inept finishing in fifth place

There was no help for Mr. Cub as they were never in the pennant race

A quarter of a century would pass before another Cub would win one more
It was second baseman Ryne Sandberg who earned it in eighty-four
He had one of those years where everything went right
And the Cubs made the playoffs, they were out of sight

Andre Dawson's first year with the Cubs was one for the ages
He had a season that proved he was worth every dollar of his wages
With 49 homers and 137 runs batted in, he was on fire all year
But, alas, he couldn't stop the Cubs from bringing up the rear

Ninety-eight was a magic year for Sammy Sosa and all of baseball
His home run chase with McGwire got him mentioned in the Hall
He hit 66 dingers and drove in an impressive hundred and fifty-eight
It's no wonder a Most Valuable Player award he did rate

Hartnett, Cavaretta, Sauer, Sandberg, Dawson, Sosa and Banks
To these seven players all die-hard Cub fans give thanks
Thanks for the memories, thanks for the records, thanks for the excitement
But most of all thanks to these seven for giving a hundred percent

CY YOUNG WINNERS

The Cy Young award is given in each league every year to the best pitcher
Receiving this award most certainly makes the recipient much richer
The Cubs have had four recipients – three starters, one reliever
Even pitching in hitter friendly Wrigley makes one a believer

Jenkins, Sutter, Sutcliffe and Maddux are the strong-armed four
Each one of them has gone down in Cubs pitching lore
And each one of them had their own unique pitching style
From speed to breaking balls to pure pitching guile

Fergie Jenkins was the Cubs first Cy Young award winner
And for all his twenty win seasons they never threw him a dinner
He won the award in seventy-one after his fifth straight 20-win season
For him not to win the award previously – there was no rhyme or reason

Bruce Sutter – the third reliever to win the award – took it in seventy-nine
The league hit only .186 against him, which was at the top of his statistical line
He became a dominant pitcher after developing a split-finger fastball
His mastery of that one pitch is what got him elected into the Hall

Rick Sutcliffe won the award in eighty-four with a unanimous vote
And the Cubs won the Division trying to overcome the superstition of the goat
Acquired at midseason, Sutcliffe won sixteen games in twenty starts
And he won all Cub fans in both their minds and their hearts

Greg Maddux won four consecutive awards, the first as a Cub in ninety-two
The Cubs had a weak pitching staff that year of which Maddux was the glue
He won 20 games that year with an earned run average of two point one eight
He went to Atlanta the next year because management didn't close the gate

Baseball is all about having fun whether you are playing the game on an amateur or professional level or just a fan. Who doesn't cheer for a pitcher on the verge of throwing a no-hit game or a slugger stepping into the batter's box late in the game with three home runs to his credit already? Here's a few short ones to enjoy that help tell us what baseball is all about.

TAKE ME OUT TO A BALL GAME

The words from the famous song ring loud and clear
Take me out to a ball game for some peanuts and beer
We'll scream and yell for our home team and root for a win
And if by chance they happen to lose it would be a mortal sin
We'll boo the visiting team and razz the umpires 'til the last out
We'll have a great time because that's what baseball is all about

THE BULLPEN?

Why do they call it the bullpen?
Shouldn't it be called the pitcher's den!
Relief pitchers hang out there all game long
They don't come alive until things go wrong

BARE-HANDED CATCHER

Silver Flint was a catcher who caught bare handed
Now, how stupid was that to be perfectly candid?
He broke every joint in all of his fingers
Foul tips must have been real stingers

DIZZY QUOTE

The Lord had his arm around me alright
Lik'd to choke me, held me so tight
When I'd get in trouble and have serious doubt

He'd pat me on the head and I'd get an easy pop out

THE MAYOR OF WRIGLEY FIELD

Hank Sauer was the Cubs premier slugger from fifty through fifty-five
This was the period of time just before Ernie Banks would arrive
His home run blasts onto Waveland had residents bearing a shield
He became so popular he was dubbed the Mayor of Wrigley Field

While with the Cubs Sauer hit 198 home runs in six and one-half years
When he went to St. Louis in fifty-six Cub fans shed a lot of tears
They should have renamed Waveland Avenue Hank Sauer Drive
For he alone – with his prodigious blasts – kept Cubs baseball alive

PAFCO IS NUMBER ONE

Andy Pafco was a star on the '45 team and a Cubs' all-time favorite
He played center between Lowery and Nicholson and was a natural fit
Playing centerfield for the Cubs in those days was no trip to the beach
Because he would have to get balls the other guys could never reach

The Topps Trading Company was so enthralled with his popularity
In their '52 inaugural set he was card number one instead of the likes of Joe D.
During the Cubs portion of his career, Andy Pafco had quite a great run
And today, that Topps card is worth five thousand dollars in near mint condition

1984

When George Orwell wrote the novel 1984 he forgot one thing
The Rick Sutcliffe and Chicago Cubs great summer wing ding
At six-foot-seven, Rick was an imposing figure on the mound
When the Cubs traded for him nobody imagined he was Cy Young bound

In '84 Sutcliffe was sixteen and one and took the Cy Young with a unanimous vote
He led the Cubs to a conference championship in an attempt to break the curse of the goat
His accomplishments that year will go down in Chicago Cubs lore
And we'll all remember the great summer of nineteen-eighty-four

BILLY BUCKS

Bill Buckner is known mostly for his World Series error and that makes me mad
He was a great fielding first baseman and just one error doesn't make him bad
Buckner has a .990 fielding percentage six years out of seven with the Cubs
That would mean you could count on one hand the number of his flubs

Buckner played for the Cubs from seventy-seven through eighty-three
During that era he was their most consistent player and an offensive key
While with the Cubs he hit over three hundred four times with one batting crown
So whenever his name appears I think Billy Bucks and wear a smile not a frown

Nicknames were a huge part of baseball in the old days. Most of them didn't make any sense to the average fan but to the players those nicknames were significant and important. Usually there is a story behind those nicknames, some very unique. Every team has had their share of players with nicknames. The Cubs with their greater than 130 year legacy had a number of players with unusual and interesting nicknames. Let's start with that and then deal with some old time nicknames that you will find rather peculiar.

CHITOWN NICKNAMES

Ever wonder where nicknames come from?
Some are ingenious and others pretty dumb
Cubs' players have had some names that are off the wall
Let's look at some of them and I know we'll have a ball

There was Wimpy, Jittery, Cupid and Brakeman
And Catfish, Popeye, Blue and Spider Man
Some very familiar ones were Sarge and Hippo
Along with The Hawk, The Penguin and Rainbow

Death to Flying Things was a 19th Century shortstop
And legendary Cap Anson was also known as Pop
Other old timers were Jiggs, Fido, Dandelion and Topsy
And there was Prunes, Orator and Grasshopper but no Turvy

How nervous was Phil Collins who was nicknamed Fidgety?
How fashionable was Tom Parrott also known as Tacky?
How about names like Sweetbreads, Trolley Line and Bubbles
And The Vulture, Swish, Old Hoss, Highpockets and Pickles

Other old timers were Little Eva, Bald Eagle and Peaceful Valley
Let's not forget Mr. Cub, The Crab, Wild Thing and Big Daddy
The mad men, Mad Dog, Mad Monk and the Mad Russian
There are many others but that's enough Cub nickname fun

NICKNAMES OF THE 1800'S

Nicknames of the nineteenth century were a bit flamboyant and weird
Except for a mustache players were clean shaven so nobody was nicknamed The Beard
Let's start with a couple of Billy's, not goats but Sliding Billy and Pigtail Billy
There was The Old Woman in The Red Cap, how's that for being silly

The Junkman was a garbage collector in the off season
Deaf and dumb players were called Dummy for habitual reason
Some weird names were White Wings, Peach Pie and The Apollo of the Box
Can someone please tell me what kind of names were these for baseball jocks

There was Sure Shot, Scissors, The Magnet and Old True Blue
How these guys got their nicknames I don't have a clue
Pete Browning was The Gladiator and Ed Morris was Cannonball
At least with names like that those men could stand tall

There was Grin, Ice Box, Whoop-La and Move Up Joe
I would have wanted to watch these guys from the front row
Razzle Dazzle was Con Murphy's unique nickname
That was probably is only claim to fame

Some flamboyant names were The Steam Engine and Grasshopper Jim
Those nicknames must have been thought up on a whim
The Little Globetrotter was the nickname given to Billy Earle
Was it because he travelled the world in a whirl?

NICKNAMES OF THE 1900'S

The turn of the century brought about nicknames even more amazing
Some of them were so eccentric that they were actually dazzling
Kid Elberfeld had the hot and spicy nickname The Tabasco Kid
If I had a nickname like that I would have run away and hid

Some of the nicknames were akin to animals in the zoo
Like Rabbit, Chicken, Turkey Mike, Iron Horse and Kangaroo
There was Wagon Tongue, Little All Right and The Human Mosquito
Now there's a group of really strange names and now you know

Pitcher Earl Moore threw sidearm so he was nicknamed Crossfire
After pitching 14 years the hitters were glad to see him retire
Then there was The Dixie Thrush, The Piano Mover and The Hoosier Thunderbolt
Just trying to remember those names would give your brain a booming jolt

As the century moved on the player's nicknames became less bold
With names like Dizzy, Daffy and Ducky they finally struck gold
These were names the fans could remember and correlate too
When you think about it, it was something the players had to do

There were names like The Man, Yogi, Babe, Muddy and Pepper
Also there was Country, Specs, Spud, Rube, Chick and Ripper
Of course there were the familiar names like Red, Slim and Whitey
Along with Buzzy, Buster, Duffy, Ping, Rube, Doc and Blondy

Now, it's the Twenty-First Century and I don't like what I see
No more Mr. Cub or Dizzy, Daffy and Ducky to bring us glee
The progression of nicknames for players has pretty much come to a halt
They've taken the fun out of the game with no clue who's at fault

Trivia is an important part of baseball. I haven't figured it out but I am sure there are well over a million baseball trivia questions. No one knows the answers to all of them. How could they when they don't know all of the questions. However, baseball trivia can be amusing, entertaining and mostly a whole lot of fun. When you put it into poetry it can be delightful and fascinating. Read on and you'll see what I mean.

TRIVIA TIME #1

It's time for some Chicago Cubs trivia so let's see what you know
For your convenience you can find the answers somewhere below
A few of the questions will be fairly easy but most will be moderately tough
So don't attempt to play the game unless you are an expert trivia buff

To help build your confidence let's start with a fairly easy one
Up until what year did the Cubs play all their home games under the sun?
Who did the Cubs pick in the 1998 amateur draft in the first round?
He's still playing but to be sure he is not Hall of Fame bound

The first draft was in sixty-five with the Cubs picking at number six
Can you name the pitcher they chose who never fit into their mix?
How many Cubs have had All-Star game-winning hits and can you name them?
Who was the Cubs pitcher on the night Koufax threw his perfect game gem?

In the early sixties the Cubs had a catcher named Barragan
What was his first name? It was one that you'll never hear again
When it comes to the World Series the Cubs have played in more than one
Can you name the player who hit the Cubs first World Series home run?

The correct answer to the first question was nineteen eighty-eight
If you got it right we've got you hooked – you took the bait
Corey Patterson was chosen by the Cubs in 1998 with their first pick
In sixty-five the Cubs picked a kid named James, first name Rick

Three Cubs have had All-Star game winning hits – Santo, Hickman and Madlock
Koufax' opposing pitcher was Bob Hendley who gave up only one base knock
Barragan's given first name was Facundo but he went by the name Cuno
In 1908 Joe Tinker hit the Cubs' first series home run and now you know

More trivia later. I've got a few more poems about my beloved Cubs and then I promise you won't have to put up with any more - at least not for awhile.

GO, CUBS, GO

It's been more than one-hundred years since the Cubs won a championship
But the true fans keep coming out to the park and yelling, "Go, Cubs, Go"
They've had some famous managers during this time, even 'Leo the Lip'
That still hasn't got them a crown, but the fans keep yelling, "Go, Cubs, Go"

There has been a number of Hall of Famers that have made the fans proud
Even that hasn't got them a crown, but the fans keep yelling, "Go, Cubs, Go"
The fans came out to see these stars and they would yell and scream out loud
But to no avail 'cause the team was a flop, but the fans keep yelling, "Go, Cubs, Go"

As the years have passed the die-hard Cub fans have grown quite weary
But they still come out to Wrigley in droves and keep yelling, "Go, Cubs, Go"
Then that thing that happened in 2003 made every Cub fan's eyes a bit teary
But the fans still support their beloved team and keep yelling, "Go, Cubs, Go"

Now it's time for Cub fans to forget about the past and look toward the future
Keep attending games and rooting for the Cubs by yelling, "Go, Cubs, Go"

Because deep in our hearts we know that a championship is near, that's for sure
So keep the faith Cub fans and continue to cheer and yell, "Go, Cubs, Go"

THE '08 CUBS

The Chicago Cubs won the World Series in Nineteen Hundred and Eight
They were the first team to win the Series two years in a row, they were great
It's a belief in some circles because of this the Gods of baseball set down a curse
It would be one hundred years or more before winning again, nothing would be worse

The 1908 team had great pitching and that is what led them to the crown
With the likes of Ed Reulbach, Jack Pfeister, Orval Overall and Three-Finger Brown
They had miniscule ERA's and were all born to pitch, not just throw
In another era they would have easily mowed down Murderer's Row

Jimmy Sheckard, Solly Hofman and Wildfire Schulte manned left, center and right
Their speed and base running was legendary and their fielding was out of sight
The infield was manned by Tinker, Evers and Chance with Steinfeldt at third
Anyone trying to hit a ball past them soon found out that idea was absurd

As usual Johnny Kling was the catcher for the Cubs that year
He handled that veteran pitching staff without peer

The Cubs won the National League championship that year by one game
They played Detroit in the Series and in five games the Tigers they were able to tame

One hundred years later – 2008 – the Cubs has championship aspirations
They had the pitching, the hitting and the means to challenge all game situations
They proceeded to lead the league in games won to prove their worth
They went into the playoffs with the attitude that they ruled the Earth

Just like the 1908 team, they had the pitching that could make hitters look silly
The rotation was made up of Zambrano, Dempster, Harden, Marquis and Lilly
Geovany Soto handled the catching chores and was a rookie sensation
His power with the bat and defense behind the plate was an inspiration

The 2008 outfielders were Jim Edmonds, Kosuke Fukudome and Alfonso Soriano
The infielders were Aramis Ramirez, Derek Lee, Mark DeRosa and Ryan Theriot
The bench was well manned by Daryle Ward, Reed Johnson and Henry Blanco
And the bullpen aces Carlos Marmol and Kerry Wood were always ready to go

The fans were excited, their enthusiasm was busting out with joy
Cub fans around the world were like kids with a new electronic toy
But something happened – all of a sudden the Cubs didn't hit, field or pitch

Leaving everyone – players and fans – with that same old nasty itch

Baseball games are won or lost on the field of play. Manager's decisions win very few games. Pitching, hitting and fielding are what baseball is all about and the player performances are what determine wins and losses. The next segment is devoted to the players. Of course, there have been way too many players throughout history to address them all so I have selected a small number of players from every era and every position and embrace their careers in poetic verse. Since a baseball game starts with the ball in the pitchers hand I will start there.

DOMINATING BOB

One of the fiercest competitors in all of baseball was Bob Gibson
He'd brush back a hitter high and inside just to create some fun
Hitters knew that the next pitch could be coming high and inside
That's why digging into the batter's box was like committing suicide

When Gibson pitched his objective was to dominate them
And just about every game he pitched was a real gem
Of course bitter rivalries always brought out the best in Bob
His determination to win was the most important part of his job

Just seeing Gibson on the mound gave hitters the chills
Just watching him pitch gave Cardinal fans thrills
With every pitch he would get meaner and more intense
You would pity the guy who might hit one over the fence

In 1968 he won both the MVP and Cy Young award
His pitching that year was as sharp as a double-edged sword
He set a National League ERA record that year
Just something else for National League hitters to fear

His pride is what built his character and success
When it came to winning he would accept nothing less
His achievements were rewarded upon his election to the Hall
He knew that his career was immortalized when he got the call

MR. SENATOR

Jim Bunning's great pitching career almost never got off the ground
The Tiger's changed his delivery and it created disaster on the mound
Jim threw with what they call three-quarters sidearm
When they changed his delivery it caused great harm

Jim threw two no hitters with one being a perfect game
Those two performances helped him get into the Hall of fame
When he threw his perfect game Jim had seven children with more on the way
It just so happened that that perfect game was thrown on Father's Day

During his playing career Jim was not a very likable sort
It was said that's the reason he didn't get much offensive support
His teammates even let it be known that they didn't like him
He didn't care about that as long as he got respect - that was Jim

He spent most of his sixteen year career with the Tigers and the Phillies
Jim was a strikeout pitcher which means he usually gave hitters the willies
For all the years that he pitched he was never on a team that won a pennant
After his playing days he went into politics and was elected to the U.S. Senate

DIZZY

Jerome 'Dizzy' Dean was one of the most colorful players in the history of baseball
He also formed one of baseball's all time sibling pitching combos with his brother Paul

When he took the mound he was determined to win and have lots of fun
And he was the last National League pitcher to win 30 games in one season

Dizzy was known for his peculiar antics which is what inspired his nickname
But it was his performance on the field that brought him the most fame
As a member of the Gashouse Gang his persona and ability made him their 'Ace'
Dizzy loved to talk and could tell the wildest, unbelievable stories with a straight face

He had an injury-shortened career when he was hit with a batted ball off his toe
He came back too soon before he was healed and that caused him considerable woe
When his playing career was over he went into baseball game broadcasting
Even tho' he butchered the English language his memory will be ever lasting

Hollywood thought so much of his career they made a movie about his life
Dan Dailey played the role of Dizzy Dean and Joanne Dru played his wife
He was elected to the Hall of Fame in '53 a year after the film was shown
And being the braggart he always was he let the prestigious award be known

QUIZ

Dan Quisenberry was a relief pitcher in the '80's with pin point control

As a closer for Kansas City throwing nothing but strikes was his goal
During a 12-year career his wild pitch count was an incredibly low four
A miniscule total like that has been written into baseball lore

Regarding fewest walks per nine innings amongst the leaders he's right there
In 1,043 innings pitched he unintentionally walked 92 – a feat very rare
When asked for his autograph he was very approachable
When it came to conversing with people he was very comfortable

Most people remember him as being brilliant, a bit quirky and funny
If salaries were where they are today he would have made lots of money
After his baseball career 'Quiz' sat down and wrote poetry
I'm sure he found it enjoyable and tranquil just like me

A quotable character he once said, "I've got a delivery in my flaw"
Never considered for the Hall of Fame he was one of the best that I ever saw
Tragedy struck when he was diagnosed with brain cancer in ninety-eight
He died that year at age 45, and many have asked why was this his fate?

ROTTY

Marv Rottblatt was a pitcher who was small in stature but big in heart
Before his professional career 'Rotty' had to learn that pitching was an art
He was born and raised in Chicago, Illinois which was also my home town

His major league pitching career wasn't distinguished but he never got down

He pitched for his home town White Sox but his development was slow
In fact he had a very high earned run average three years in a row
After retirement from baseball 'Rotty' went into life insurance sales
When he sat down to sell you a policy he was tough as nails

I had the pleasure of meeting 'Rotty' when he sold me a life policy
I pulled out a baseball card of him and he politely signed it for me
A college in Minnesota named an intramural softball league after him
So he was honored and recognized that his baseball career wasn't all that dim

IT'S ALL WET

Gaylord Perry was one of the craftiest pitchers that there ever was
All of baseball knew that he threw a spitter – at least that was the buzz
Years later after retiring he admitted that he used to doctor the ball
Even knowing this the Baseball Writers of America elected him to the Hall

Perry pitched for twenty-two years and amassed three hundred and fourteen wins
Hitters might have fared better if they would have come to the plate wearing swim fins
He wasn't your quintessential athlete and he couldn't hit a lick
Perry used to psyche out hitters so the spitter wasn't his only trick

His two hundred sixty five losses are the most of any pitcher in the Hall of Fame
That might be because he wasn't able to doctor the baseball in every game

In 1983 he retired to his North Carolina farm to grow peanuts and tobacco

He also held autograph sessions at many a sports card show

I met him briefly at a sports card show and we both had a good laugh

I was standing nearby when a lad handed him a ball for his autograph

As Perry handed the ball back I said, "It might be slippery don't let it fall on the floor"

Gaylord looked at me, smiled and said matter of factually, "I don't do that anymore"

OLD HOSS

In 1884 Charles 'Old Hoss' Radbourn had the greatest year a pitcher ever had

He won 59 games as he pitched almost every day but in those days that was the fad

He was the best pitcher of his era and if he were pitching today he'd be regarded as an 'Ace'

He pitched so much because his team the Providence Grays was involved in a pennant race

1884 was also the first year that overhand pitching became legal
That may have attributed to Radbourn's statistics being so regal
It's assumed 'Old Hoss' got his nickname because he was a workhorse
He pitched 678 innings in 1884 to live up to that nickname of course

Also in 1884 'Old Hoss' won the pitching triple crown
In Providence, Rhode Island he was the toast of the town
He won 309 games in twelve years so he was hard to beat
And his lifetime ERA was 2.68 which was quite a feat

Someone once coined the phrase, "Catcher's equipment is the tools of ignorance." It probably came from the notion many years ago that a smart player would not play such a grueling position. This, of course is a complete misnomer. For a catcher 'tools of ignorance' would be to wear no gear at all. Actually, the catcher has more tactical and strategic knowledge than any other player on the team. In fact, many of them have outstanding managerial careers after hanging up their so called 'tools of ignorance'.

JOE AND THE MIC

Joe Garagiola lived on the same block as Yogi Berra when he was a youth
After playing baseball he had a distinguished career in the broadcast booth
Joe's playing career wasn't that distinguished over nine seasons
In 676 games in only drove in two hundred fifty five runs

During his career Joe was traded four times which is above the norm
He once quipped, "I thought I was modeling everyone's uniform"
Joe had an almost thirty year association with NBC television
He was elected to the announcer's wing of the Hall of Fame before he was done

You might say Joe was a character of the game from the stories he revealed
He probably has a collection of secretive stories that he's kept concealed
Most of the stories he told were interesting, funny and a real treat
Like the one – because of Berra – not being the best catcher on his street

SQUATTER'S RIGHTS

Tony Pena caught while squatting on his left leg with his right leg stretched out
When I first saw him I did a double take and thought what's this all about
His catching style was unconventional and unorthodox to say the least
Although medium in stature his unique style made him a catching beast

I used to think that every game I watched behind home plate he had squatter's rights
His style did not hamper his catching ability and it brought the position to new heights
With runners on base he would abandon the squatting and use the conventional style
He had a strong arm and this would allow him to throw base stealers out by a mile

His squatting gave pitchers a low strike zone which makes a lot of sense
Tony was cheerful and good-natured but when game time came he was intense
He hit a respectable two-sixty for his career which lasted eighteen years
He was an exceptional defensive catcher and was revered by his peers

After his playing career was over Tony took to managing
But because of circumstances it became a short fling
He is currently a bench coach for the New York Yankees
Where he can sit and rest his sore and worn out knees

WAVING IT FAIR

Carlton Fisk's 'waving homer' in the World Series gave him instant glory
But his career was a whole lot more than that so there's more to his story
'Pudge' as he was known played his entire career for the Red Sox and White Sox
During his incredibly long 24-year career he had plenty of hard knocks

His early years with the Boston Red Sox were his most prolific
But in seventy-two and seventy-five he was absolutely terrific
However, it was his long productive career that got him elected to the Hall
He hit 376 home runs with a good number of them over that monstrous wall

In 1981 he signed with the White Sox and became an instant hit in Chicago
No one knows for sure but it's a good guess he changed teams for the dough
In his later years his offense tailed off but that made a lot of sense
However, the one thing that never changed was his solid defense

He hit 214 home runs while toiling for the Sox on Chicago's south side
While playing in Boston he only gave 162 balls a long ride
In eleven years in Boston he hit a very respectable two-eighty-four
At the end of his career the White Sox took an unusual way to show him the door

IT'S GOOD TO BE ALIVE

'It's Good to be Alive' is Roy Campanella's inspirational autobiography

It's about his dealing with the fact that never walking again was a possibility
'Campy' was paralyzed from an auto accident in the winter of fifty-eight
He regained use of his arms and hands and wrote the book about his shocking fate

Campanella was one of the players that helped break the color barrier in baseball
His career was so good that in nineteen-sixty-nine he was elected to the Hall
One of 'Campy's' early coaches was the legendary catcher Josh Gibson
Between Gibson and Biz Mackey they worked him hard and took away the fun

The long hours and hard work ended up paying off for 'Campy'
As his hitting and fielding made a whole lot of Dodger fans happy
Three times he was elected Most Valuable Player as proof of his dominance
That's something because very few other players have earned such prominence

In 1953 'Campy' hit 41 homers and led the league as he drove in 142 runs
He also threw out 54% of stolen base attempts to prove his arms were like guns
'Campy' eventually overcame the bitterness of his fate and stopped pouting
Once he did that the Dodgers gave him a job in community relations and scouting

EL SENOR

Al Lopez managed for 15 years and his teams always had a winning record

That's why his winning percentage as a major league manager has soared
He's fourth on the list behind Joe McCarthy, Frank Selee and John McGraw
Lopez was an outstanding catcher which educated him how to manage with nary a flaw

'El Senor' as Lopez was known started his baseball career at age sixteen
He broke into the majors in '28 and the number of years he played was nineteen
His offensive stats were consistent year in and year out
But it was his defense that shined without a doubt

In 15 years he only managed two teams in the majors, Cleveland and Chicago
All the years he managed the great Yankee teams of the fifty's were his major foe
His home town of Tampa honored him with a ball field in his name
And his career was revered when he was elected to the Hall of Fame

RAIN DELAY PERFORMER

Rick Dempsey came from a show business family so he was born to entertain
And that he did when he ran around sliding into bases while a game was delayed by rain
The rain came down in buckets and the fans enjoyed the stunt while they waited
It was darn funny at the time and over the years many times it's been imitated

Dempsey had a twenty-four year major league career and many wonder why
Although he was an excellent fielder just watching him hit would make you cry

Rick played for seven teams during his career, some of them twice
Which means he was well respected as a catcher to be precise

Dempsey played in four different calendar decades, one of 32 players to do so
His most valuable asset to a team was the way he made the locker room glow
After retirement he took to coaching and then baseball game broadcasting
He still works as a studio analyst because his knowledge of the game is everlasting

MR. BASEBALL

Bob Uecker was given the name 'Mr. Baseball' by Tonight Show host Johnny Carson
The smartest thing Uecker ever did was to quit baseball and seek another occupation
The highlight of his career was hitting a home run off of Sandy Koufax
Having an undistinguished career he retired before they could give him the axe

In 1971 he became the radio announcer for Milwakee Brewer game broadcasts
He became famous saying "Get up! Get up! Get outta here! Gone!" describing home run blasts
Uecker started doing a number of beer commercials as his career continued to grow
It was in one of these commercials that he coined the phrase, "I must be in the front row."

We all know he also became an actor and starred in the TV series Mr. Belvidere
But he always returned to his home town Milwaukee, the city known for its beer

He had a very short major league baseball career as it only lasted six years
That's probably because whenever he came to bat he heard nothing but jeers

His lifetime batting average is two hundred which is equal to the Mendoza line
That's the main reason he was relegated to a backup role which with him was just fine
One thing about his outstanding broadcasting career that's a shame
He has yet to be elected to the broadcasting wing of the Hall of Fame

Besides the pitcher and catcher, the first baseman encounters the most action of all the other infielders. As a rule he has more putouts from balls put in play in a game than any other player on the field. First basemen are usually power hitters but some of the best average hitters have been first basemen. One thing that is required from a first baseman is good defense. I have selected a very interesting group of first basemen to keep your interest.

THE NATURAL

Bernard Malamud's "The Natural" was based in part on the Eddie Waitkus incident
An obsessed female fan shot Waitkus in a Chicago hotel room in a bizarre event
While trying to remove the bullet Waitkus almost died in the operating room
It took some time for Eddie to heal enough so his baseball career could resume

His career started out very good but after the shooting it was never the same
Of course, everyone figured the incident in the hotel room was to blame
His batting average hovered around three hundred before his fight to stay alive
But he ended his career hitting a respectable two-hundred and eighty-five

Waitkus suffered from post-traumatic stress disorder as a result of the shooting
This generated his clinical impairment in significant areas of functioning
He became an instructor at a baseball camp and the work he performed was gratifying
At age fifty-three he developed cancer and had to quit the camp because he was dying

BIG KLU

Ted Kluszewski was a tall, heavy man thus the nickname 'Big Klu'
In fact he was so big he would often block a base runner's view
'Big Klu' had a 4-year span when he hit 171 home runs
It was due to his arms being like a set of big guns

He cut off the sleeves of his uniform to free up his swing
It helped him immensely and he became a home run king
The Reds front office was upset that he altered the uniform
They claimed that doing such a thing was above the norm

Besides hitting for power 'Big Klu' had eight seasons that he hit over three-hundred
That's probably why his number was retired and he was an all-time Cincinnati Red
Besides being a productive hitter 'Big Klu' had excellent defensive skills
Day in and day out he provided his fans with an abundant of baseball thrills

THE HUMAN RAIN DELAY

Mike Hargrove's antics when batting got him the nickname, 'The Human Rain Delay'
He would do so much fidgeting and stepping out of the batter's box it would stop play
Could you imagine if he did all that fidgeting while facing Gibson or Drysdale
He would have gotten a bundle of high and inside fast balls without fail

Mike played a power position but only hit 80 home runs in a 12-year career
But his other statistics were good enough to help his team year after year

He won the American League Rookie of the Year Award in
   seventy-four
Because of his batter's box fidgeting he will be a part of baseball
   lore

After retiring as a player Mike stayed in baseball and took to
   managing
All baseball fans are thankful he didn't teach his players about
   fidgeting
He had a successful managing career that included one World
   Series trip
However he wasn't able to win that elusive championship

DR. STRANGEGLOVE

Dick Stuart's fielding was so bad they called him Dr. Strangeglove
With every ball hit or thrown his way teammates would ask for
   help from above
Irritating fielding at first base wasn't his only bad stat
During his career he struck out once every four times at bat

One day Stuart picked up a hot dog wrapper blowing toward him
   and took it out of play
He got a standing ovation from the crowd as it was the only thing
   he picked up all day
Stuart's career ended before the American League passed the
   designated hitter rule
He could have been a DH and burned his glove - to Dick Stuart
   that would have been cool

Looking on the bright side of Dr. Strangeglove's career
He hit sixty-six home runs in the minors one year
In a ten-year major league career Stuart's home run total was two-
   hundred twenty-eight
If his fans are watching for his election to the Hall of Fame they've
   got a long wait

THE FIRST GREAT SLUGGER

First baseman Dan Brouthers' Hall of Fame career began in eighteen-seventy-nine
'Big Dan' was not an instant success and early in his career he rode the pine
Once he put it all together he was one of the best of his period
When it came to driving in runs and hitting homers he was a stud

Brouthers delighted the fans with on-field antics during a game
They would be frowned upon today and put a player to shame
He was the first true character of the game and just wanted to entertain
His antics were harmless and funny and didn't cause fellow players any pain

Dan was a big man for his time and was the first pure power hitter
When he'd hit a long home run it would usually make the pitcher bitter
Like so many other players from his era not much is known about his personal life
He did have an Irish setter named Kelly but unknown if he ever had a wife

It's believed the dog was named after King Kelly, Dan's friend and teammate
Dan would bring Kelly to the games and he would sit in the dugout and cooperate
After retirement his friend John McGraw gave him a job with the Giants baseball club
For twenty years he has varied duties from security to operating the whirlpool tub

BIG AND STRONG

Joe Adcock was a big and strong man and he could hit a baseball a long way

If a pitcher made a mistake and grooved one Joe would put it out
   of play
He played his best years with Mathews and Aaron on the
   Milwaukee Braves
The three of them hit so many home runs the sports writers gave
   them all kinds of raves

Joe was such a powerful man he would give pitchers nothing but
   trouble
In 1954 Adcock had a game to remember when he hit four home
   runs and a double
The next day a pitcher named Gomez tried to hit Joe with a pitch
   high and inside
Waving his bat Joe chased Gomez into his locker room where he
   would hide

Joe hit three-hundred and thirty-six home runs with some of them
   being Ruthian blows
With the possibility of Joe hitting one back through the box
   pitchers had to stay on their toes
Besides being an ideal hitter for his position his fielding ability
   was absurd
Upon retirement his .994 all-time fielding percent for first basemen
   was third

DOUBLE X

Jimmie 'Double X' Foxx was one of the top ten power hitters in
   the history of the game
'Double X' hit 534 home runs in his career off of pitchers who
   have only themselves to blame
If I were a pitcher in that era I would never throw him a strike
   especially with men on base
He drove in more than nineteen-hundred runs in his marvelous
   career so I rest my case

Jimmie is the greatest right-hand hitting first baseman that ever
    played the game
He was an easy first ballot choice for his election to the Hall of
    Fame
He runs a close second to Lou Gehrig as the greatest first baseman
    of all time
'Double X' won three Most Valuable Player Awards when he was
    in his prime

Foxx made his major league debut with the Athletics at a very
    young age
He was seventeen which made it hard to make an impact on the big
    stage
Two years later he was a starter at first base and his majestic career
    began
It was a short time later that he became the Philadelphia Athletics
    main man

Jimmie played in the same era as Ruth, Gehrig, and Hornsby
Unfortunately he didn't receive the notoriety as those three
'Double X' played most of his career in Philadelphia and Boston
He jumped around at the end and even played for the Cubs before
    he was done

The second base position is the mirror image of the shortstop position, and of course, vice versa. The main difference is turning the double play. The second baseman has to turn his body to throw the ball to first base after the putout at second while the shortstop is usually facing in that direction. Fans and baseball writers and experts have offered their opinions on who is the best second baseman of all time – or even the top five or ten. With the likes of (in alphabetical order) Roberto Alomar, Eddie Collins, Nap Lajoie, Joe Morgan and Jackie Robinson to name a few, it would be hard to pin point which was the greatest because they all played in different eras. They all had the same qualities that identify the importance of a Hall of Fame second baseman. Each of them could field, hit, run, and most important they all had great knowledge of the game and the position they played. Not to embroil a debate about which one was the greatest, I will ignore these great ballplayers and address others who contributed their talents to the position.

POOSH 'EM UP

Tony Lazzeri was a member of the New York Yankees famed Murder's Row
He batted second in the lineup with Ruth, Gehrig, Meusel and Dickey to follow
Tony didn't have the power his mates had but he was a good hitter in his own right
He hit eighteen home runs his rookie year so from time to time he'd hit it out of sight

Lazzeri's unusual nickname came from a mistranslation of a phrase Italian fans would shout
It was translated as 'Poosh 'Em Up' but the correct translation should have been 'Hit It Out'
One minor league season Tony hit sixty homers and drove in two-hundred twenty-two runs
The RBI total is still a record at any level so a bat in Tony's hands was like two smokin' guns

A number of teams passed on signing him because he was diagnosed with epilepsy
It was their loss as the Yankees signed him and got a ballplayer with outstanding ability
Lazzeri once drove in eleven runs in a game which is an American League record
Tony kept driving in runs all day long and all day long the crowd roared

After retirement Lazzeri briefly took up minor league coaching and managing
It didn't work out and at the young age of 42 epilepsy was the cause of his dying
Lazzeri's place in history should be he was one of the greatest Yankees of them all
The Hall of Fame Veteran's Committee thought so when they elected him to the Hall

SPIRIT AND DETERMINATION

"Give me eight players with spirit and determination and I'll give you a winning team"
That's an Al Lopez quote that was never put to use but he was probably right on the beam
When Lopez made that statement he was alluding to his second baseman Nelson Fox
He and Fox toiled together as manager and second baseman for the Chicago White Sox

Early in his career 'Nellie' was a part-time player because he lacked in abilities
He worked hard, had inspired spirit and determination and learned his baseball A-B-C's
He was rewarded with a career that exceeded everyone's expectations including his

His hitting, base running and fielding around second base made him a wiz

He was the best second baseman in the American League during his time with the Sox
'Nellie' batted over three-hundred six times and he was a tough out when in the batter's box
Fox' legacy is that hard work, spirit and determination will improve your game
In his case it was enough to get him elected to the baseball Hall of Fame

MAZ

Bill Mazeroski is best known for his walk-off home run to win a World Series game seven
His ninth-inning blast at Forbes Field put Pirate fans in a frenzy thinking they were in Heaven
It suddenly ended one of the most exciting games in World Series history
But Mazeroski's career was more than a home run that gave him glory

'Maz' played his entire career in Pittsburgh and is one of their all-time greats
About everyone he played with rate him as one of their favorite teammates
He is rated by many as one of the greatest fielding second baseman of all time
He liked diving for balls and coming up with a uniform full of dirt and grime

'Maz' won eight Gold Glove awards which is proof of his defensive ability
It was his defensive prowess that got him elected to the Hall by the Veteran's Committee

The '60 World Series was one of the most exciting and warranted that type of finish

Watching an historic ending like that is every baseball fan's wish

GENTLEMAN BID

'Bid' McPhee was the nineteenth century's best fielding second baseman

In fact, his bare-handed fielding expertise delighted every baseball fan

Yes, you read that right, 'Bid' played bare handed 14 of his 18 years

Besides having a pair of sore hands he had the admiration of his peers

'Bid' was just a nickname as his given first and middle names were John Alexander

How he got his nickname is not known but it could be his father was an auctioneer

He was a true gentleman of the game even though he played in a rowdy age

Some of the players were so unruly and violent they should have been put in a cage

'Bid' played his entire 18 year career with the Cincinnati franchise

His fielding skill got him elected to the Hall which is no surprise

Shortly after retiring he managed the Reds for a short term

After two years he was fired because his losing record made ownership squirm

THE BELLIGERENT LITTLE MAN

'Kid' Gleason was called 'The Belligerent Little Man' by columnist Warren Brown

Could be because wherever he played or managed he thought he owned the town

Although Gleason was short in stature he was an aggressive ball player
He was an acceptable second baseman but started his career as a pitcher

'Kid' got his nickname because he was the smallest kid in his neighborhood
Being small didn't let it affect him as he became a pitcher that was pretty good
He won 138 major league games including 38 in eighteen ninety
During his time playing second based he hit around two-sixty

Gleason was the manager of the 1919 Black Sox which was his biggest claim to fame
He noticed something was wrong when the Sox lost the World Series' first game
If he were still alive today, Gleason would ardently insist
The 1919 White Sox team ranks as the best on his list

THE MECHANICAL MAN

Charlie Gehringer was dubbed 'The Mechanical Man' for good reason
Just wind him up on opening day and he runs on and on all season
Gehringer was a flat, un-exciting player thus giving the name a second meaning
He never changed his dull expression on the field no matter what the inning

Another reason for 'The Mechanical Man' was his durability for consecutive games played
He had two streaks of more than 500 games attesting his love for the game was top grade
His manager said, "Charlie would say 'Hello' on opening day and 'Goodbye' on closing day"
He would continue, "In between he would hit three-fifty" so Charlie sure earned his pay

81

Actually, Charlie didn't hit three-fifty every year but he came close to it

Every day, without changing expression, he would hit and hit and hit

Gehringer didn't just hit as his fielding around second base was sublime

In fact, he was one of the best fielding second baseman of all time

He was elected into the Hall of Fame in 1949 because of the numbers he posted

It's too bad no one thought of it but he would have been a great one to be roasted

Charlie reluctantly took the job of Tigers General Manager in nineteen-fifty-one

The Tigers had a bad team and for Charlie trying to rebuild them was no fun

THE BRAT

I'm not sure but it seems that most of the characters of the game played second base

They pulled some bizarre and sometimes fantastic antics and did it with a straight face

The definition of a brat (Eddie Stanky) is: an annoying, spoiled or impolite child

That surely defines the unusual on-field activities of Stanky to put it mild

'The Brat' was famous for getting on base a bunch besides the wild antics

Every year he would draw over 100 walks to get on base and have his kicks

What Stanky lacked in ability he made up for it with enthusiasm and desire

He came to play every day and played the game as if his pants were on fire

- Durocher said of him, "He can't hit. He can't field. All he can do is win"
- What Leo forgot to say was 'when he takes the field he makes things happen'
- After retirement 'The Brat' took up managing at the major league level
- It didn't last long as he couldn't win even if he had made a deal with the devil

The shortstop is the most important infielder because statistics show more batted balls are hit in his vicinity of the field than anywhere else. The more range and quickness a shortstop has the more valuable he is to his team, defensively. I believe there are three defensive categories for shortstops. By coincidence they all start with the letter S. They are sure-handed, slick-fielding and short-term.

The sure-handed shortstop has limited range but fields everything hit at or near him with few errors. The slick-fielding shortstop has unlimited range and is able to make unbelievable defensive plays. The short-term shortstop is slow afoot and has minimum skills.

I'm going to try and cover a wide range of shortstops, so here we go.

LITTLE LOUIE

If Ozzie Smith is the best defensive shortstop ever than Luis Aparicio isn't far behind
In fact, 'Little Louie' might have been better and this is not just a state of mind
When the '59 White Sox won the pennant they were led by Fox and Aparicio
But it was 'Little Louie' with his speed and defense that made the team go

'Little Louie' had the most speed and range for a shortstop that I have ever seen
Of all the slick-fielding shortstops that have come along he still is the dean
Just about every year he would lead the league in stolen bases
It seems he would steal four or five bases before he tied up his laces

Looie was born in Venezuela, a hotbed for Major League shortstops

In fact, very few shortstops that came from there were big league flops
Looie's phenomenal fielding made up for his inadequacies with the bat
His defensive prowess made the crowd stand up and cheer and tip their hat

In 1984 - after six years of eligibility – Louie was finally elected to the Hall of Fame
What took them so long? But then some Baseball Writers don't understand the game
Louie went into the Hall the same year as another shortstop named Pee Wee
The number of Hall of Fame shortstops currently stands at twenty-three

HUGHIE

Hughie Jennings is one of the Top 10 shortstops when all the reasoning is done
He is the only shortstop in history to hit over .400 for an entire season
He hit .401 before the turn of the century in eighteen-ninety-six
That same year he was hit by a pitch 51 times – ouch, he sure took his licks

The next two years he was hit forty-six times each year to seal his fate
Did they have a batter's box back then or did Jennings stand on the plate?
Jennings, along with Honus Wagner were the best shortstops of their period
Although Wagner was a better hitter, in the field Jennings was a real stud

Just like Wagner and Nap Lajoie, Jennings worked in the mines as a young man

Determined to leave a life of mining, Hughie molded his future with a plan
During the off-season to mold his future he took law classes at St. Bonaventure
After baseball he became a lawyer to complete his life adventure

Hughie was a skinny man, his face was loaded with freckles and he had bright red hair
His best friend was Wee Willie Keeler and when they got together they made quite a pair
Jennings election to the baseball Hall of Fame was an easy decision
Because he played the shortstop position with exquisite precision

BUCKY

Russell Earl "Bucky" Dent was born in 1951 under the name Russell Earl O'Dey
Bucky grew up in the south but came to the big cities in the north to play
Bucky started his career with the White Sox but found it a tough way to go
He was expected to fill the shoes and follow in the footprints of Luis Aparicio

He is most famous for his end of season tie-breaker home run against the Red Sox in '78
He was playing for the Yankees and the home run sent their rivalry into a furious state
When compiling a list of the most famous home runs in baseball history
Not including Bucky's blast on that list would be a major travesty

GREAT HANDS

Many players and managers have said Roy McMillan had the
  greatest hands they ever saw
He could go to his left and go to his right and field just about every
  ball without a flaw
Roy played ten of his sixteen years in the major leagues with the
  Reds of Cincinnati
He was a popular player and a fan favorite with a lifetime batting
  average of .243

In1957 Roy and six of his teammates where elected as starters to
  the All-Star Game
But his top honor was in '71 when he was inducted into the
  Cincinnati Reds Hall of Fame
He finished his playing career with the New York Mets and the
  Braves of Milwaukee
Then he took up coaching and managing for a while but it just
  wasn't his cup of tea

TRAMS

Alan Trammell played for the Detroit Tigers all twenty years of his
  career
At the shortstop position during that time he had 'nary a peer
His .285 lifetime batting average is one of the highest for a
  shortstop
And his one hundred eighty five home runs showed his bat had a
  lot of pop

For many years Alan and Lou Whitaker were the Tiger's second
  base combination
In fact, they went down as one of the greatest second base duos
  before they were done
Alan made his major league debut in '77 when he was only
  nineteen years old

It's fair to say from all the successful years he had that the Tiger's struck gold

Trammell was elected or named to six American League All-Star teams

With a statistical resume like his he should be in the Hall of Fame it seems

However, the powers that be that have a vote seem to ignore his name

Let's hope that someday they'll realize Trammell belongs in the Hall of Fame

Third Basemen do not have to be fast. However, they must be quick in many different ways. They must have quick feet so they can field hard hit balls to their left or right. They need quick hands and reactions to hard hit line drives and ground balls hit right at them. And, of course they must be quick thinkers so they throw to the right base depending upon the situation.

Most third basemen are known for being an offensive power hitter in the middle of the lineup. A third baseman who has both requirements – hitting and fielding - is truly a valuable member of his team. Here are a few of the great ones.

THE BEST OF THE BEST

When ranking baseball's all-time best third basemen Mike Schmidt is number one
He hit with power and his fielding was outstanding and his arm was like a gun
Mike's career started off slow but it didn't take him long to become a legend
His perseverance and superior work ethic proved he wouldn't break or even bend

Mike hit more than five hundred home runs over the wall
But that's not the only reason he was elected to the Hall
How about his career RBI's that totaled fifteen-hundred and ninety-five
Which proved with runners on base his bat would come alive

Schmidt played all eighteen years of his career for the Philadelphia Phillies
When analyzing his awards and numbers he had to give pitchers the 'willies'
Mike appeared in twelve all-star games and his Silver Slugger awards numbered six
 He won ten gold glove awards and three National League MVP's among the mix

THE HEBREW HAMMER

Al Rosen was signed by the Cleveland Indians as a free agent in 1942
In 1953 he won the American League MVP award and was the team's glue
In '53 he hit forty-five home runs and had 145 runs batted in
Both of those totals led the league by a huge margin

He banged out 201 hits for a .336 average that year – both were career highs
Then in the following year he led the American League in sacrifice flies
In the five year period from 1950-54 his runs batted in average was 111
Another amazing statistic in his rookie year his home runs totaled thirty-seven

Al was the top Jewish baseball player in the decade of the fifties
Following in Greenberg's footsteps who was the best in the forties
He retired after ten years of playing because of chronic back trouble
When he went down so did the Indians bursting their bubble

MORE HOME RUNS THEN AARON

For Milwaukee the legendary Henry Aaron hit 398 home runs in all
But Eddie Mathews topping that with 452 is one of the reasons he's in the Hall
In fact, Eddie was one of the most prolific home runs hitters in history
Hitting more than 30 home runs nine consecutive years is just part of his story

He led the National League in home runs with 47 in '53 and 46 in '59

He had other yearly totals of 41, 40, 39 and 37 which is mighty fine
Eddie was named to 12 all-star games and received MVP votes in 10 years
One of the top five third basemen of all times he had few peers

In '53 he had the best year in history of baseball for a 21-year-old player
He is the third baseman on the all-star team of best young players ever
Mathews was elected to the Hall of Fame in 1978, ten years after retirement
They finally elected him when his vote totaled almost eighty percent

MR. UNDERRATED

Darrell Evans was underrated by many because he did so many things well
No, he didn't do anything great but his consistency would help teams gel
His major league career spanned a total of twenty-one years
During that time he didn't receive many jeers nor did he get many cheers

Darrell showed up every day and played to the best of his ability
He played the game hard and to win which is what the fans came to see
He did lead the league once as he hit 40 home runs in nineteen-eighty-five
Darrell hit 414 career home runs so that wasn't the only time his bat was alive

Evans was one of the top fielding third baseman during his playing time
He usually finished the day with his uniform full of dirt and grime
After his long and distinguished career was over and done

It's a shame that he never got any Hall of Fame consideration

CHIPPER

Larry Wayne Jones Jr. was a third baseman who played hard and was solid as a rock
He got the nickname Chipper from his dad because he was a 'chip off the old block'
He was the number one overall pick in the 1990 Major League draft
The Atlanta Braves drafted him because they hungered for his craft

Chipper was a switch hitter who was equally adept at both sides of the plate
Throughout his career there were many games that his bat would dominate
His accomplished career statistics would surely backup that reasoning
And in 1995 his career was highlighted with a World Series ring

His other awards include a batting championship and National League MVP
His batting champ year he hit .364 when he went on a dominating hitting spree
Chipper was an eight time all-star and two time silver slugger award winner
When eligible for the Hall of Fame he should be a first time ballot victor

Outfielders can generally be placed into one of three classifications. Good hitter, challenged fielder – Good fielder, challenged hitter – Good hitter, good fielder. Of course there have been a few outfielders who have been challenged hitters and fielders but they don't last too long.

The good hitter, challenged fielder is usually a slow footed power hitter who doesn't hit for much average and even covers less ground in the outfield. This type of lumbering player is usually installed in left field. Home run hitters like Ralph Kiner, Hank Sauer and Dave Kingman come to mind as fitting this description.

The good fielder, challenged hitter usually plays center field. His profile is that he can cover a lot of ground in the outfield and make spectacular catches at times. However, he has trouble getting on base consistently. When he does, he usually has speed and can disrupt a pitcher's concentration.

The good hitter, good fielder of course is a blessing and every team wants one or two or more of them. The exceptional ones throughout history are players such as Willie Mays, Mickey Mantle, Ty Cobb, Joe DiMaggio and current young stars Mike Trout and Bryce Harper.

Here is a cross section of outfielders with a variety of baseball skills.

SHOELESS JOE

Joe Jackson was one of Major League baseball's all-time best
He could run, hit, field, throw and played the game with zest
Joe got his nickname from playing one day with blisters on his feet
He removed his shoes and went to bat without missing a beat

Jackson couldn't read nor write and it became an issue all of his life
In fact most of his memorabilia items have been signed by his wife
His legendary feats with the bat held other players in awe
And his quickness running out a triple broke every speed law

Everyone knows his career was cut short by that Black Sox scandal thing
If not for that he could have been baseball's all-time hitting king
To his dying day he claimed his innocence and didn't go for the dough
However he never answered the written question, "Say It Ain't So, Joe"

THE LOUISVILLE SLUGGER

Pete Browning was not only a great hitter he was one of baseball's characters of the game
One of the nineteenth century's top hitters it's a travesty he's not in the Hall of Fame
Pete was known as 'The Louisville Slugger' thus the name for the bat he used
Being uneducated he did some things on and off the diamond that left everyone confused

Pete had this superstition at the end of every inning he would touch the third base bag
At the end of an inning one day an opponent took the base away and left nothing to tag
Pete chased the culprit all around the field but never could catch the thief
At bat that inning he saw the base was there and he ran to tag it – 'O what a relief

Although he was a great hitter his catching fly balls gave him trouble
His manager thought a cigar store Indian would do better and hold runners to a double
Once, eating dinner in a restaurant he saw a fly in his soup and threw a fit
"Don't worry, Pete," the waiter - a baseball fan - said, "you won't catch it

Then there was the time he was told that President Garfield was assassinated
"Oh really, and which team did he play for," he stated
Pete had a lot of health problems that started when he was a young lad
He was deaf and that caused him to have headaches that really hurt bad

THE CUBAN COMET

Saturnino Orestes Armas Minoso Arrieta was Major League Baseball's first black Cuban
That name was much too long so he simplified it to Minnie Minoso to the delight of every fan
He was nicknamed 'The Cuban Comet' because of his speed and daring base running
He was also an accomplished hitter and fielder and was very adept at bunting

Cleveland signed him as a third baseman but couldn't give him any playing time
Traded to the White Sox he became a fan favorite and joined their sublime
Minoso led the American Leagues in stolen bases, doubles and triples
Some of his extra base hits made outfielders look like cripples

Minnie appeared in games over five decades only the second player to do so
And had many outstanding years playing for the White Sox in Chicago
Not too long ago I was perusing the names in Baseball's Hall of Fame
I couldn't fine Minnie's name at all – now that's a crying shame

BASEBALL TRIVIA #2 – OUTFIELDERS

Who was the first batter in the first World Series game that took place in 1903?

What outfielder was both a high school and 1969 Mets teammate of Tommy Agee?

What Chicago Cub outfielder said he would rather play baseball than eat?

Who is the only player to capture an MVP award as a rookie – quite a feat?

What Outfielder is a second cousin to shortstop Bert Campaneris?

What former baseball manager was best friends with Roger Maris?

Who was the former outfielder that tried to steal home while coaching third base?

What well traveled outfielder was tagged with the nickname 'suitcase'?

Who replaced Shoeless Joe Jackson in left field for the 1920 White Sox?

What Braves' center fielder of the 1950's was as quick as a fox?

Who was the Red Sox outfielder who quit at a young age from fear of flying?

What outfielder was teammates with Rudy York and would join him in drinking?

Ginger Beaumont of the Pittsburgh Pirates was the World Series first hitter

Cleon Jones was Agee's high school and 1969 Mets teammate amongst all that glitter

That Chicago Cub that hungered for baseball more than food was Andy Pafco

Fred Lynn was the rookie who won the AL MVP award when he put on quite a show

Bert Campaneris' second cousin is Jose Cardenal – the one with the wacko hair

Whitey Herzog and Roger Maris were best friends and they made quite a pair
George Van Haltren was the third base coach that attempted that bizarre folly
Harry Simpson was nicknamed suitcase after the character in Toonerville Trolley

One of baseball's all-time best base runners Bibb Falk replaced Shoeless Joe
It was Bill Bruton who made the Braves of the fifties go, go, go
Even a hypnotist couldn't help Jackie Jensen overcome his flying fear
Pete Fox and Rudy York could drink all night and put away cases of beer

LEGENDS IN THE OUTFIELD

Legendary outfielders can be remembered by only saying their last name
Those guys were so good it was a given they'd make it to the Hall of Fame
The best of the best were Mays, Williams, DiMaggio, Cobb, Mantle, Aaron and Ruth, of course
I used the Encyclopedia of Baseball as my statistical source

Other legends include Clemente, Speaker, Musial, Ott, Yaz, Jackson, and Kaline
And lest not forget Puckett, Wilson, Robinson, Snider, and Griffey Jr. players so fine
Every one of them had baseball skills that were out of this world and simply divine
Fans would flock to the park to see them play under the lights or in the sunshine

At the top of the list is a guy named 'Babe', oh what a hitter he was

With every home run he hit the fans would cheer and shout and create such a buzz
Then there's the legend that Ruth saved baseball after that Black Sox scandal
You know the one, it was started by White Sox first baseman Chick Gandil

The following is a recap in no particular order of the careers of the rest of the best of the best
They all represented the game with utmost respect and played the game with remarkable zest
They showed up every day with pride and enthusiasm to play the game they love
Every one of them had tremendous skills with both the bat and the glove

When Henry Aaron hit the home run that broke Ruth's record off lefty Al Downing
The fans stood up and cheered and were all smiling except for the pitcher, he was frowning
Aaron was a scrawny kid that just kept hitting home runs year after year
So that home run was not the only highlight of his magnificent career

Joe DiMaggio had a great career topped off with his 56 game hitting streak
That happened early in his career way before he really hit his peak
DiMaggio made such an impact as a Yankee early on he was nicknamed 'Joltin Joe'
His lifetime 361 home runs and .325 batting average caused many a pitcher's woe

Ty Cobb was known to have a surly temperament and an aggressive playing style
His career lasted twenty-four years and there were a number of records he did compile

Most impressive of his feats was to accumulate more than four thousand hits
And his fifty-four steals of home drove defenses out of their wits

Boston Red Sox left fielder Ted Williams is the last of the four-hundred hitters
Every time he strode to the plate that year he gave the pitcher the jitters
Many baseball aficionados have called him the greatest hitter of all time
As a marine aviator during World War II he lost years during his prime

'The Commerce Comet' Mickey Mantle's baseball skills were a site to behold
He could hit, run and field with the best of them or so it's been told
He hit 536 home runs over a career that spanned eighteen years
320 of them came over eight seasons in a row that's matched by very few peers

Baseball is not an easy game except for guys like Willie Mays
He was so good that he could beat you in so many ways
His 660 home runs were second to Ruth when he retired
Just watching him play the game – players and fans admired

Now let's review the careers of the other outfield legends and their feats
They all could have been immortalized in poetry by Shelley and Keats
Those guys are dead so their poetic verse on the legends will never be
They'll have to settle for whatever lyrical words come from me

Hack Wilson holds the season record for runs batted in at 191
Just watching him hit that year must have been a lot of fun
He got the nickname Hack because his body was reminiscent of a taxi cab
He was short and stocky but very muscular without much flab

Kirby Puckett was built along the same lines as Wilson but not as strong
Every game he would fill the stadium and he usually would thrill the throng
Even tho' he was short and stocky around the bases he could really fly
His career was cut short when diagnosed with glaucoma in his right eye

Edwin Snider played for the Dodgers and was nicknamed "The Duke of Flatbush'
Whenever 'The Duke' had a good year the Dodgers would make a World Series push
In the mid-fifties he had five consecutive seasons with forty home runs or more
Whenever he came up to bat during those years he would make the crowd roar

Al Kaline won the American League batting title when he was twenty years old
He was one of the Detroit Tigers' greatest all-time hitters or so it's been told
He played his entire career for the Tigers - all twenty two years
When he retired Tiger fans everywhere shed thousands of tears

Carl Yastrzemski was chosen to replace Ted Williams – if that was possible
Yaz as he was known went on to have a career that was pretty remarkable
He is a member of the three thousand hit club and won the triple crown
During the length of his illustrious career he owned 'Beantown'

Tris Speaker was a great center fielder and won many hitting titles during his career
Every day he would show up at the ballpark and put his game into high gear

He was an intricate part of the 'Million Dollar Outfield' of the Boston Red Sox
Tris has more doubles than any other player in history as part of his 3,500 plus base knocks

Stan Musial was such a great and consistent hitter that he was nicknamed 'Stan the Man'
When the Cardinals needed a big hit it was Stan who came through and delighted ever fan
His 3,630 hits was why he was able to carve out a lifetime batting average of .331
He set multiple National League hitting records before his great career was done

On three successive pitches Reggie Jackson hit home runs in a World Series game
The achievement came in game six of the '77 Series to underscore his fame
Because of that remarkable feat he became known as 'Mr. October'
He hit 563 home runs in his career and they came between April and September

Mel Ott led the National League in home runs six times even though he was small
He hit 511 career home runs while weighing 170 pounds and only five-foot nine-inches tall
Since 1959 the National League home run champion is honored with the Mel Ott Award
Ott had outstanding statistics because he handled his bat like a Musketeer's sword

Ken Griffey Jr. was a second generation outfielder and was born to play baseball
It's just too bad that he played for teams that weren't good enough to play in the fall

During his career he was one of the most exciting and prolific hitters around
When pitchers knew he was coming to bat they didn't want to take the mound

Frank Robinson won the MVP in both leagues the only one to attain such a feat
He is also the first African-American to serve as manager which is really neat
Frank was a triple crown winner and a member of two World Series winning teams
For everything he accomplished in his career for him it wasn't as hard as it seems

Roberto Clemente was the first Latin American and Caribbean player elected to the Hall of Fame
He was one of baseball's all-time greats and lost his life at age 38 – what a shame
Among his many honors he won twelve consecutive gold gloves and four batting championships
He was a great fielder with a strong arm and with a bat in his hands he always took good rips

IN CLOSING

Training camp is over and the baseball season is starting like every other spring
Every team starts on an even keel with expectations of winning a World Series ring
Ruth, Gehrig, Cobb, Wagner, Mathewson and Alexander are no longer here
Now we have Trout, Harper, Cabrera, and Kershaw so don't shed a tear

Some of the old timers think the game has changed and have let it be known through the press
Throughout history nothing stays the same including the game of baseball – it's called progress
Every year a rules committee makes rule changes and sometimes they're not so subtle
And there are always those players and fans that will hold major changes in rebuttal

It's up to you fans to get out and support the game, the players and your favorite team
Shout and root for them to win and get to the World Series – every fans dream
There isn't an excuse to not attend 'cause there's always a game from ocean to ocean
And always remember every move in our great pastime of baseball is poetry in motion

Reference Credits:

Baseball-reference.com
The Encyclopedia of Baseball
The New Bill James Historical Baseball Abstract
Wikiepedia, the free encyclopedia

www.ingramcontent.com/pod-product-compliance
Lightning Source LLC
Chambersburg PA
CBHW071306040426
42444CB00009B/1896